Immortality

Immortality

Josiah Royce

Planktos Press

Published by Planktos Press.
Sydney, Australia.
www.planktospress.com

Copyright © 2023

Paperback ISBN: 978-1-922931-00-9
Hardback ISBN: 978-1-922931-02-3
eBook ISBN: 978-1-922931-01-6

Immortality was originally published in *William James and Other Essays on the Philosophy of Life (1911)* by The Macmillan Company, New York.

All questions about Immortality relate to some form of the continuance of human life in time, beyond death. All such questions presuppose, then, the conception of time. But now, what is Time? How is it related to Truth, to Reality, to God? And if any answer to these questions can be suggested, what light do such answers throw on human's relation to time, and on the place of death in the order of time?

Secondly, all questions about Immortality relate to the survival of human personality. But, what is our human personality? What aspect of a human do you want to have survive? In considering these two sets of questions, I shall be led to mention in passing several others, all of which bear upon our topic.

My honored colleague, Professor Münsterberg, in his recent little book on "The Eternal Life," has raised in a somewhat novel form an old issue regarding the metaphysics of time, and has applied his resulting opinion to our problem of immortality. The real world, he has said, - the world of the absolute, is an essentially timeless world a world of meanings, of ideal values a world where there is no question of how long things endure, but only a question as to what value they have in the whole of real life. In this genuinely real world of ideal values everything has eternal being in accordance with its absolute worth. A value cannot be lost, for it belongs to the timeless whole. But the ordinary point of view, which so emphasizes time, as most of us do, is merely a quantitative view - a falsification, or at least a narrowing, of the truth - a transformation of reality a translation of its meaning into the abstract terms of a special set of concepts useful in our human science and in our daily business, but not valid for the student of real life. Matter, indeed, endures in time; but then matter is a conceptual entity, a phenomenon, a creation, of the scientific point of view. A human endures in time while their body lives; but this is only the human as viewed in relation to the clocks and to the calendars - the phenomenal human - the human of the street and the marketplace, of the psychological laboratory and of the scientific record, of the insurance agents and of the newspapers. The real human whom you estimate and love is not this phenomenal human in time, but the human of will and of meaning, of ideals and of personal character, whose value you acknowledge. This real human is what they are worth. Their place in the world is determined not by the time during which they endure, but by the moral values which they express, and which the Absolute timelessly recognizes for what they eternally are. This real human does not come and go. They are. To say that they are immortal is merely to say that they have timeless value. And to say that is to express your love for them in its true meaning.

Hence, as Professor Münsterberg holds, the whole problem about immortality is falsely stated in popular discussion. Revise your view of time. See how time is but an appearance belonging to the world of description; that is, the world of conceptual clocks and calendars; and then the real human is known to you, not as temporally outlasting death, but as, in their timeless ethical value, in the real world of appreciation, deathless. For they belong to the realm of meanings; and the timeless Absolute of real life neither waits for them to come, nor misses them after their death as one passed away, but acknowledges them in their true value as what they are, the real person, whose eternal significance as little requires their endless endurance in the unreal conceptual time of the calendar and of the clock makers, as this same significance requires them to have a taller stature than they have in the equally unreal conceptual space of the metric system and of the tailor's measuring tape.

So far my colleague, as I venture to restate his view. I do not agree with him in the way in which he has formulated and applied this view. Yet I think that

Professor Münsterberg is at least in one respect justified in printing his essay. He is justified, namely, in calling our attention to the fact that, in order to discuss immortality exhaustively, we must include in our discussion some view of the sense in which time itself is a reality. And I also think that my colleague's view of time, although not mine, contains an important element of truth. Let me try to suggest what this element is.

I need not say to theologically trained readers that you cannot well conceive of God without supposing the Divine Being to be otherwise related to time than we men just now are. To view the Deity as just now waiting, as we wait, for the vicissitudes of coming experience that are floating down the time stream towards him, to conceive the divine foreknowledge merely as a sort of clever computation of what will yet happen, a neat prediction of the fortunes that God has yet to expect - well, I cannot suppose any competent theologian to be satisfied thus to conceive of the divine knowledge of time, or of what time contains. If God is merely the potent computer and predicter, whose expectations as to the future have never yet been disappointed, then he remains merely upon the level of a mighty fortune teller and fortune controller a magician after all. And not thus can you be content to conceive of the divine omniscience. If the question arose: Why might not God's foreknowledge some day prove to have been fallible? Why might not revolving time force upon him unexpected facts? - then you would certainly reply: "If God, as God, absolutely foreknows, that means, properly viewed, not merely that he skilfully anticipates, or even that he mightily controls fortune, but that time, present, past, future, is somehow his own, is somehow at once for him, is an eternal present for which he has not to wait, a total expression of his will which he not merely remembers or anticipates, but views in one whole, *totum simul*, as St. Thomas well insisted."

God's relation to time cannot, then, be merely our own present human relation. We expect what is not yet. But if God is God, he views the future and the past as we do the present. And in so far Professor Münsterberg's view is indeed well founded. The lasting or the passing away of things as we view them does not express the whole divine view of them. What has, for us men, passed away, is, for the divine omniscience, not lost. What is future is, from the divine point of view, a presentation. Time is in God, rather than is God in time. Some such view you surely must take if God is to be conceived at all.

But if God views facts as they are, this indeed implies that death, and the passing away of humans, and the lapse of countless lives into what we call the forgotten past, cannot really be what we take these things to be an absolutely real loss to reality of values which, but for death, would not become thus unreal. As a fact, I do not doubt that the least fact of transient experience has a meaning for the divine point of view a meaning which we very ill express when we say of such a fact: "It passes, it is done, it is no more." In reality that is, from the divine point of view - there can be no absolute loss of what is once to be viewed as real at all.

Now so far, using, to be sure, for the moment, theological rather than my colleague's metaphysical terms, I suggest a view about time which is obviously close to that which Professor Münsterberg emphasizes. Nevertheless I do not agree with him that, by means of such considerations, we can completely define the sense in which humans are immortal. I turn, then, from this first naturally vague effort to hint that our human view of time is inadequate, and that even our present brief lives have a divine meaning which no human view of their transiency exhausts, I turn, I say, from this glance into general theology, back to the problem about time, as we men have to conceive time. We talk of tomorrow, of the time after death, of the future in general. In that future, we say, we are to live or not to live. Every such formula, every such hypothesis, presupposes some sense in which our words about the future can have truth, even today presupposes then some doctrine about what time is, and about how the past and future are related to the present. We must therefore ask again, but now in a more definite way, What reality has time, whether for the universe or for us?

It requires but little reflection to see that, in our ordinary speech about time, we are accustomed to use obscure, if not contradictory, language. We often ascribe true reality to the present only, and speak as if the past, as being over and done with, had no reality whatever; while the future, as yet unborn, we hereupon view as if it were also wholly unreal. The present, however, this only real region of time, we often speak of that as a mere point, having no duration whatever. Yet in this point we place all reality; and meanwhile, even as we name it, this sole reality vanishes and becomes past. Time, however, if thus defined, consists of two unreal regions, which contain together all duration all that ever has been or will be; and time, in addition to these, its unreal halves, contains just one real instant, which itself has no duration, and which is thus no extended part of time at all, but only a vanishing presence. Thus, after all, there remains, when thus viewed, no real region in time at all. Nothing is; all crumbles. Such a view has only to be explicitly stated in order to be recognized as inadequate; as a fact, such a view is a mere heap of false abstractions. Moreover, we ourselves not only frequently assert, but almost as constantly deny, this interpretation of time. For the past we view, after all, as a very stern and hard reality. What is done, is done. The past is irrevocable, unchangeable, adamantine, the safest of storehouses, the home of the eternal ages. Moreover, you can tell the truth about the past. Hence the past is surely not unreal in the sense in which fairyland is unreal. A human who practically treats the past as unreal, becomes *ipso facto* a liar; and you might in fact define a false witness as a human who tries to make the past over at will, not recognizing its stern and unalterable truth. On the other hand, the future indeed is not thus irrevocable; but it has its own sort of very potent and recognizable being. You constantly live by adjusting yourself to the reality of the future. The coal strike threatens. You wish that your coal bins, if they are not full, were full. For next winter, after all, is a reality. Thus, then, the two regions of time, the past and future, are not wholly unreal. For the truthful witness the past is a reality. For the faithful maker of promises the future is a reality. As for the present, after all, are many dreams less real than is the mere present? Fools live in the present, and dream there, taking it to be the real world. But whoever acts wisely, knows that the present is merely their chance for a deed; and that the worth of a deed is determined by its intended relations to past and future.

Not the present, then, of our flickering human consciousness, is the temporal reality, so much as are the past and the future. Life has its dignity through its bearing upon their contents and their meaning.

We see from these illustrations, I hope, that much of our common speech about time is belied by our practical attitudes towards time. Truthful reports and promises, serious deeds and ideals, prudence and conservatism and enterprise, all unite to show us that the reality of time is possessed especially by its past and its future, over against which the present is indeed but vanishing. And now what, after all, do such illustrations teach us regarding the true meaning of our conception of time?

I answer at once, dogmatically, but, as I hope, not without some suggestion of the reason for my answer: Time, to my mind, is an essential practical aspect of reality, which derives its whole meaning from the nature and from the life of the will. Take away from your conception of the world the idea of a being who has a will, who has a practical relation to facts; take away the idea of a being who looks before and after, who strives, seeks, hopes, pursues, records, reports, promises, accomplishes; take away, I say, every idea of such a being from your world, and whatever then remains in your conceived world gives you no right to a conception of time as any real aspect of things. The time of the timepieces and of mechanical science, the time of geology and of physics, is indeed, as Professor Münsterberg maintains, but an abstraction. This abstraction is useful in the natural sciences. But it has no ultimate meaning except in relation to beings that have a will, that live a practical life, and that mean to do something. Given such beings, it can be shown that they need the conception of the time of mechanics or of geology in order to define their relation to nature. But apart from their needs, time is nothing. The time regions, already mentioned in this account, get their distinct types of reality solely from their diverse relations to a finite will, and, for us, to our own finite will. The past is that portion of reality where, to be sure, deeds also belong; but these past deeds are presupposed by my present attitude of will as already, and irrevocably, accomplished facts. As such they are the acknowledged basis upon which all present deeds rest. That is, then, what I mean by the past, viz. the presupposed and hence irrevocable basis on which my present deed rests. I say, "So much is done." The will, therefore, presupposing the past, asks, "What next?" and is ready to decide by further action. The future is equally definable solely in terms of the will. The future is the region of the opportunity of the finite will. The future also, indeed, contains its aspect of destiny - as, for example, next winter's chill. But it likewise contains the chance of deeds yet undone, and so incites the will. As for the present, it is the scintillating flash of the instant's opportunity and accomplishment. It too is meaningless except for the deed, be this deed a mere act of attention or an outward expression. In terms, then, of my attitude of will, and only in such terms, can I define time, and its regions, distinctions, and reality.

Time then is, I should say, a peculiarly obvious instance of the necessity for defining the universe in idealistic terms that is, in terms of life, of will, of conscious meaning. Burdened as we all are by the mere concept of the time of the clock makers and of the calendars, by the equally conceptual time of theoretical physics and of daily business, we are prone to forget that it is the human will itself which defines for us all such concepts, which abstracts them from life, and which then often bows to them as if they were indeed mere fate. If you look beneath the abstractions, you find that time is in essence the form of the finite will, and that when I acknowledge one universal world time, I do so only by extending the conception of the will to the whole world. If I say: "There is to come a future," I mean merely: My will acknowledges deeds yet to be done, and defines as the future reality of the universe a will continuous with my will - a world will in whose expression my present deed has its place. The unity and continuity of the time of the universe are definable only through the practical relation of my will to this world will. My deed has its place in the system of the world's deeds. The will that is yet to be expressed in the future is inseparable in its essence from the will which even now, and in my present deed, acknowledges this future as its own. As appears from these forms of expression, I am in philosophy an idealist. This is no place to set forth lengthy arguments for idealism. I have to sketch and to speak dogmatically. But the conception of time is peculiarly good as an illustration of the need of idealism.

My result is, so far, that time is indeed in definable and meaningless except as the form in which a conscious will process expresses its own coherent series of deeds and of meanings. And so, if all the finite world is subject to one time process, this assertion means merely that all our wills are together partial expressions of a single conscious volitional process the process whereby the world will gets expressed infinite forms and deeds. A complete argument for idealism would, of course, have to develop and to supplement this interpretation of time in many ways. But here is a hint of idealism.

A result so stated is, I admit, not at first sight at all decisive as to any question of personal immortality. Yet I hope that the reader will already see how a doctrine of this sort, dogmatically as I have to state it, fragmentarily as I have to suggest my reasons for holding it, must have some bearing upon the problem as to how and whether a personal survival of death is a possibility. One is too much disposed to view the time process as an utterly foreign fate, physically forced upon unwilling mortals, who can only lament how youth flies, and how the good old times come again no more, and how the unknown future, vast and merciless, is impending and is yet to engulf us. What I now point out is that all such abstract conceptions of the fatal, external, physical, inhuman, unconscious reality of the world's time process are inadequate. As we have seen, in our sketch of a few such false conceptions, they appear in various, in paradoxically conflicting forms, which sometimes treat all time as unreal except the present, and sometimes view the past and future as an iron reality of blind fate. As a fact, so I insist, we concretely know time as the form of the will. We define the time relations practically, and in terms of deeds done and to be done. If we generalize our time experience, so as conceptually to view the whole world as expressing itself in a single temporal process, our generalization means this: that the entire world is the expression of a single will, which is in its totality continuous with our own, so that the past and future of our personal will is also the past and future of this world will, and conversely.

The lesson, however, is already this: If, as is very obviously true, there was a time when I personally did not exist, then that was because the world will did not then yet need, and so did not yet involve, in its own expression, and as a part thereof, my personal deeds. If, on the other hand, the time is to come when I, in my private personality, shall have become extinct, that can be only because the world will as a whole, after my passing away, is thenceforth to presuppose all of my personal deeds as irrevocably done, and is to have no longer any need to include my further choices. Assume, for the moment, that this is to be the case. This world will, however, is in any event not foreign in nature to my own will, but is continuous therewith; just as continuous, namely, as the real time of my own consciousness is continuous with the real time of the universe. If I die, then, and finally cease, that will be because a will a conscious will - a will essentially continuous with my own

- a will now expressed in my consciousness, but sure to be forever expressed in some consciousness - a will that now includes all my hopes and my meanings must someday come to look back upon my personal life as an expression no longer needed. My extinction, then, if it comes, will be at all events a teleological, not a merely fatal process an inner and purposive checking of the very will which now throbs in me a checking which will also be a significant attainment not a blind passing away, due to the mere fate that, in time, all becomes unreal. "Our life," said wondrous old Heraclitus, "is the death of gods; our death is the life of gods." And Heraclitus meant by these words that if indeed all passes away, and if we pass too, that can only be because that very divine life which now lives in us will, living in other divine forms, accomplish the very meaning which it now partially accomplishes in us, by expressing itself otherwise, and yet as the very life which is now ours. "For we are also his offspring."

Considerations such as these are indeed but highly fragmentary. They certainly do not by themselves give any adequate notion of immortality. They have been emphasized by many thinkers who thereby meant merely to make light of personal permanence. Nevertheless, to conceive time as the form of the will, and universal time as the form of the world will, and our lives as linked to a conscious world will by precisely as close a link as binds the time of our consciousness to conceive of all this, I say, is to be helped to a sort of introduction to a more definite view of our problem. In time you are at any rate not lost as the snows are lost when they melt; or engulfed as the mountains are engulfed when they are washed away and sink, as sediment, into the sea. For the world time is also the time of your consciousness; and, in precisely as genuine a sense, the world will is your will. If you ever become extinct, that will occur only as a single deed, or as a partial expression, becomes extinct for the doer who, presupposing that very deed, bases their own further expression upon the acknowledgment, the valuation, and the memory of the past deed itself. The question whether such extinction will occur at all thus gets its proper teleological formulation. You will die, not as blind fate determines, nor merely because time flies: you will die, if at all, because the world will needs no more of your personal deeds, except in so far as they are henceforth merely pre-supposed.

So far, then, I suggest what might be called a voluntaristic theory of the time process. I understand, I may say, that Professor Münsterberg would in large measure agree with even this account of the time relations as due to, as expressions of, the significant attitudes of a world will. The point where my colleague and I are at variance is now ready for a clearer statement than is the one so far given in this discussion. The difference relates to the way in which this entire will process, this whole expression of significant activities in the universe, appears when viewed, so to speak, *sub specie eternitatis*; that is, in its wholeness, as God must be conceived to view it or as any one ought to view it who does not confine himself to the abstract concepts of the clock makers and of the calendars, but who considers real life as it genuinely is, in its veritable meaning.

The time process is the form of the will. Past and future differ as deeds yet to be done differ from presupposed and irrevocable deeds. The present is the vanishing opportunity for the single deed. The time distinctions, then, are relative to deeds and to meanings. Grant all this for a moment. What follows? Does it follow that whoever views the world life as it truly is, sees the whole world as a timeless totality, consisting simply of meanings, of acts, of will attitudes, whose relations are not temporal, but significant? Does it follow that endurance in time is no test of the worth of a personality, any more than colossal stature is needed as an attribute of a great personality?

I cannot agree to such a conclusion, in the form in which Professor Münsterberg states it. First, then, as to the supposed timelessness of the world of real meanings, let me use an aesthetic example. Music, which Schopenhauer called an image of the will, is in any case essentially an art that expresses beautifully significant musical meanings in temporal order. Abstract, however, from the time form of music, and what is left of any musical form whatever? If the gods listen to music at all, they must appreciate its sequences. Wherein consists, however, a true musical appreciation? Whoever aimlessly half listens to the musical accompaniments of a dance or of a public festival, may indeed be so absorbed in the passing instant's sound that they get no sense of the whole. True listening to music grasps, in a certain sense as a *totum simul*, entire sequences measures, phrases, movements, symphonies. But such wiser listening and appreciation is not timeless. It does not ignore sequence. It is time-inclusive. It grasps as an entirety a sequence which transcends any one temporal present. In this grasping of the whole of a time process one gets a consciousness of a present which is no longer merely a vanishing present, but a time-including, a relatively eternal present, in which various vanishing instants have their places as relatively present, past, and future one to another.

Well, such a view, as I take it, comes nearer to getting the sense of what real life is than does any view which considers its world merely as timeless. If, then, I try to conceive how God views things, I can only suppose, not that the absolute view ignores time, but that the absolute view sees at a glance all time, past, present, future, just as the true appreciator of the music knows the entirety of the sequence as a sort of higher or inclusive present a present in which the earlier stages do not merely vanish into the later stages, and yet, on the other hand, are not at all devoid of time relations to the later stages.

For this inclusive view, as I suppose, sees the totality of the significant deeds and will attitudes as a single life process temporal because it is both significant and volitional, and present, not in the vanishing, but in the inclusive and eternal sense present not as a timeless whole, but as an infinite sequence "one undivided soul of many a soul," one life in, infinite variety of expression.

For such a view, however, a view which is not timeless, but time-inclusive the duration of a given series of will acts, the wealth, the lasting, the variety of a distinguishable portion of the entire process, might have yes, must have a true relation to the degree of the significance which this portion of the whole possesses. A truly great work of musical art must involve a considerable sequence. Its length has a definable relation to its greatness. What is true of a work of art might be true of so much of the world life as constitutes an individual finite being. There might be significant time processes - individual lives, so to speak - whose meaning would require them to be endless, and whose place in the whole might demand that, once having appeared, they could never in the later will activities of the temporal order be ignored, but must thenceforth cooperate - the temporal will process always including amongst its deeds activities which were not only its own, but also their own.

If such individual lives, distinct in their meaning from other partial expressions of the world will, endless in their duration from some one point onwards, were actually factors in the world process, and were amongst the facts which the absolute view of real life had to include, in order to express and to find its own complete truth - how would such lives be related to the world life in its entirety? How would they be related to that absolute insight, to that divine view, which, in an eternal, that is, in a time-inclusive sense, would see at a glance the entirety of the world process?

If I try to suggest, however vaguely, an answer to these momentous questions, the reader will understand that I am merely sketching, and am not now trying to prove, what elsewhere I have discussed with tedious detail, and in a far more technical way. Here we have no time to weigh arguments pro and con. I can only outline, in a dogmatic way, my views. I merely suggest a few of their reasons.

I have spoken of a world will. I have said that to recognize, as we all do, one time process as holding for all the world, is to recognize the world will as a single volitional process in which all our lives are bound up. We are simply different modes of willing, continuously related to one another and to the total world will which throbs and strives in all of us alike, but which, in endless variety, seeks now this and now that special aim accomplishes now this and now that special deed presupposes an infinity of deeds as its own past goes onto an infinity of deeds as its future is content to be no one of us, but shows in our social life the community of our endlessly various aims, as in our individual lives it exhibits an endless variety of differentiations and of distinguishable trends of purpose. It is one will in us all; yet I have tried to show, elsewhere, that this does not deprive us of individuality. It needs our variety and our freedom. And we need its unity and its inexhaustible fertility of suggestion. We read the symbols of this inexhaustible fertility when we study nature, and when we commune with humans. We acknowledge this unity whenever we view the time of the world as one time. Our own will to live is the will of the world, conscious in us, and demanding our individual variety as its own mode of expression. We conspire with the world will even when most we seem to rebel. We are one with it even when most we think of ourselves as separate. Art, ethics, reason, science, service, all bear witness both to our unity with its purposes, and to its need that all unity of purpose should be expressed through an endless variety of individual activities.

I have thus spoken of the world

will as this infinitely complex unity in the variety of all finite wills. I have also spoken of an absolute point of view, which views this entire life of the world will as one whole. I have used theological speech, and have called this absolute point of view that of the divine being, the point of view of God. Now this is no opportunity to consider either the proofs for the divine existence or the problem regarding the nature of God. I have again to use dogmatic forms of speech. I mean by the term "God" the totality of the expressions and life of the world will, when considered in its conscious unity. God is a consciousness which knows and which intends the entire life of the world, a consciousness which views this life at one glance, as its own life and self, and which therefore not only wills but attains, not only seeks but possesses, not only passes from expression to expression, but eternally is the entire temporal sequence of its own expressions. God has and is a will, and this will, if viewed as a temporal sequence of activities, is identical with what I have called the world will. Only, when viewed as the divine will this world will is taken not merely as an infinite sequence of will activities, but in its eternal unity as one whole of life. God is omniscient, because his insight comprehends and finds unified, in one eternal instant, the totality of the temporal process, with all of its contents and meanings. He is omnipotent, because all that is done is, when viewed in its unity, his deed, and that despite the endless varieties and strifes which freedom and which the variety of individual finite expressions involve. God is immanent in the finite, because nothing is which is not a part of his total self-expression. He is transcendent of all finitude, because the totality of finite processes is before him at once, while nothing finite possesses true totality.

If one hereupon asks, Why should there be finitude, variety, imperfection, temporal sequence at all? we can only answer: Not otherwise can true and concrete perfection be expressed than through the overcoming of imperfections. Not otherwise can absolute attainment be won than through an infinite sequence of temporal strivings. Not otherwise can absolute personality exist than as mediated through the unification of the lives of imperfect and finite personalities. Not otherwise can the infinite live than through incarnation in finite form, and a rewinning of its total meaning through a conquest of its own finitude of expression. Not otherwise can rational satisfaction find a place than through a triumph over irrational dissatisfactions. The highest good logically demands a conquering of evil. The eternal needs expression in a temporal sequence whereof the eternal is the unity. The divine will must, as world will, differentiate itself into individuals, sequences, forms of finitude, into strivings, into ignorant seekings after the light, into doubting, erring, wandering beings, that even hereby the perfection of the spirit may be won. Perfect through suffering this is the law of the divine perfection.

All these assertions would need, were there time, their own defense. I do not assert them as merely my own. That they are substantially true is what the whole lesson of the moral and religious experience of our race seems to me to have led us to see. That they are necessarily true can, as I think, be demonstrated.

So much, then, for some hint as to how the temporal is, to my mind, related to the eternal.

But what, one may ask, has all this to do with deciding the problem regarding immortality? Much, every way, I reply, if you only add, at this point, a little reflection as to the second of the two questions with which this paper opened. We have studied our relation to time, and also have considered the relation of time to the divine being. But what, so we asked at the outset, is a human personality?

Incidentally, as it were, we have now almost answered this question, so far as it here concerns us.

A human personality has many aspects, psychological, physical, social, ethical. But a human is a significant being by virtue not of their body, or their feelings, or their fortunes, or their social status, but by virtue of their will. The concept of personality is an ethical concept. A human, as an ethical being, is what they purpose to be, so far as their purpose is as yet temporally expressed. So far as their will is not yet expressed, their life belongs to the future. All else about them besides their will, their purpose, their life plan, their ideal, their deed, their volitional expression, all else than this, I say, is mere material for humanhood, mere clothing, mere environment, or mere fortune. Ignorantly as they now express themself, their worth lies not in the extent of their knowledge, but in the seriousness of their intent to express themself. Are they a sinner, then they are not yet true to their own will; that is, they are not yet, in the temporal order, their own complete and genuinely ideal self. For my duty is only my own will brought to a reasonable self-consciousness, and is not an external restraint. Hence the sinner is not yet their own explicit self. Their conflict with the world is also an internal conflict an inner war with their own imperfection. But if one who appears in the outer form of human shows no sign as yet of having any personal ideal, or life plan, or purpose, or individual will at all, then one can only say, "Since here we find a seemingly blind expression of the world will, but not an expression that as yet gives an account of itself, we must indeed suppose that some form of personality is here, in this fragment of the time process, latent, but we simply cannot tell what form." In such a case we indeed call the being whom we know in our human relations a person; but he so far appears as a person by courtesy. An explicit personality is one which shows itself through deeds that embody a coherent ideal - an ideal which need not be abstractly formulated, but which must be practically active, recognizably significant, consciously in need of further temporal expression. Such an explicit personality may be that of a hero, of a saint, or of a rascal. The hero and the saint are simply personalities that are so far expressed in forms whose deeds and ideals have a truer internal harmony. A rascal is a finite personality who is, so far as their personality is yet expressed, essentially at war with themself, as they are with the world. For their deeds are opposed to their true meaning. In so far as they appear to us, as they often do, to be a contented rascal or a joyous sinner, who observes not this essential warfare with themself in just so far, I say, they are a fool, and, accordingly, in just so far they lack explicit personality; so that, when we judge them as such a joyous rascal, we know not with what personality we are dealing. But the awakened sinner, however obstinate in their wrong-doing, is a consciously tragic figure. They may also be much of a hero. We shall then admire their vigor. But they remain a warfare of ideals and deeds, and so is not yet come to themself. The true hero, the righteous human, the saint, - these are personalities on a higher level. But at no one point in time have they attained their total expression. For the dutiful will, in a finite being, is insatiable. It views itself as a dutiful will in so far as it seeks something yet to be done; and it views itself as an individual dutiful will in so far as it consciously says: "Since this is my duty, nobody else in the universe no, not God, in so far as God is other than myself - can do this duty for me. My duty I must myself do. And wherever in time I stand, I am dissatisfied with what is so far done. I must pass on to the next."

Saints and sinners, so far as they are indeed explicit personalities, that is, finite wills conscious of their own individual intent, agree in being, in the temporal world, practically dissatisfied. The righteous human is dissatisfied with their present opportunity to express their will. They need yet further future opportunities to do their duty. The conscious sinner is dissatisfied with the very will which they are at the moment trying to express. Each, as a finite being, engaged in a temporal process, is a person by virtue of their very "dissatisfactions." I refer now by the word "dissatisfaction," not to gloomy feelings, so much as to eagerness for further deeds. How we feel is a matter of fortune. How active we need to be, that constitutes our very selves, as now we are. For a finite personality, I insist, is a will to do something. So far as I have something yet to do, I am, however, dissatisfied with the past as with the present. I demand, in just so far, a future - a future in which, since I am now a sinner, at war with myself, I shall come into unity with my own will, and shall discover what it is that I am seeking - a future in which, in so far as even now I know and intend my duty, I shall further express this will of mine in the countless deeds that my personal purpose requires me yet to do.

So much, then, for a hint regarding what a finite personality is. But in view of all the foregoing, how shall we say that such a finite personality is related to the world and to God? I reply: A finite personality, as a conscious expression of the world will, is, when viewed in time, an expression of what is just now a dissatisfaction and of a dissatisfaction of this very personality with itself. In so far as consciously sinful, this personality is dissatisfied with what it so far knows about its own will; but in so far as it is a finite doer of deeds, this personality, whether just or unjust, is dissatisfied with what it has so far done to express its will. Hence it looks to the future. And our very conception of the temporal future is due to this our present active dissatisfaction.

That such dissatisfactions should be at all in the world is due, however, as we have said, to that general need which demands that the eternal should be expressed through the temporal, that the divine and absolute should take on human and fallible form, and that the infinite should be incarnate in the finite. Not otherwise than through a divine immanence, however, can I conceive all these finite forms of temporal striving to arise.

What then follows? Does not this follow at once? The finite personality can say: "In me, as now I am, God is dissatisfied with himself just in so far as now he is partially expressed in me. I am a form of that divine dissatisfaction which constitutes the entire temporal order. This is my link with God, that now I am discontent with the expression of my personality."

In me, then, God is discontented with his own temporal expression. This very discontent I myself am. It constitutes me. This individual thirst for infinity, this personal warfare with my own temporal maladjustment to my own ideal - this is my personality. I am this hatred of my own imperfection, this search for the future deed, this intent to do more than has yet been done. All else about me, fortune, feeling, hope, fear, joy, sorrow, these are accidents. These are my clothing, my mere belongings; these constitute the very wilderness of finitude in which I wander. But I - I am essentially the wanderer, whose home is in eternity. And in me God is discontent - discontent with my waywardness - discontent with the little so far done. In me the temporal being, in me now, God is in need, is hungry, is thirsty, is in prison. In me, then, God is dissatisfied. But he is God. He is absolute. Eternity is his. He must be satisfied. In eternity, in the view of the whole temporal process, he is satisfied. In his totality he attains, and he attains what I seek.

This then is, as I conceive, the situation of any finite personality. How is this divine satisfaction attained? I answer, not by ignoring, either now or hereafter, the voluntary individual expression; for it is of the very essence of personality to define its opportunity, its deed, and its meaning, as individual, as insatiable, and unique. And God, too, so defines them, if he knows what personality is. No; the divine satisfaction can be obtained solely through the deeds of the individual. No finite series of these deeds expresses the insatiable demand of the ethical individual for further expression. And this, I take it, is our rational warrant for insisting that every rational person has, in the endless temporal order, an opportunity for an endless series of deeds.

To sum up: Since the time order is the expression of a will continuous with my own, my life cannot ever become a wholly past fact unless my individual will is one that, after some point of time, becomes superfluous for the further temporal expression of the meaning of the whole world life. But as an ethical personality I have an insatiable need for an opportunity to find, to define, and to accomplish my individual and unique duty. This need of mine is God's need in me and of me. Seen, then, from the eternal point of view, my personal life must be an endless series of deeds.

This is a sketch of what I take to be

the doctrine of immortality. The reader will observe that I have spoken wholly of will, of deeds, and of opportunity for deeds. I have carefully avoided saying anything about fortune, about future rewards and punishments, about future compensations for present sorrows, about one's rights to meet again one's lost friends, about any of these better known popular aspects of our topic. As a fact, I pretend to no knowledge about my future fortunes, and to no rights whatever to demand, as a finite personality, any particular sort of good fortune. The doctrine of immortality is to my mind a somewhat stern doctrine. God in eternity wins the conscious satisfaction of my essential personal need. So much I can assert. But my essential personal need is simply for a chance to find out my rational purpose and to do my unique duty. I have no right to demand anything but this. The rest I can leave to a world order which is divine and rational, but which is also plainly a grave and serious order.

www.ingramcontent.com/pod-product-compliance
Lightning Source LLC
Chambersburg PA
CBHW070339120526
44590CB00017B/2953